Charming Paris

Adult Coloring Book

Inspire Creativity, Relief Stress

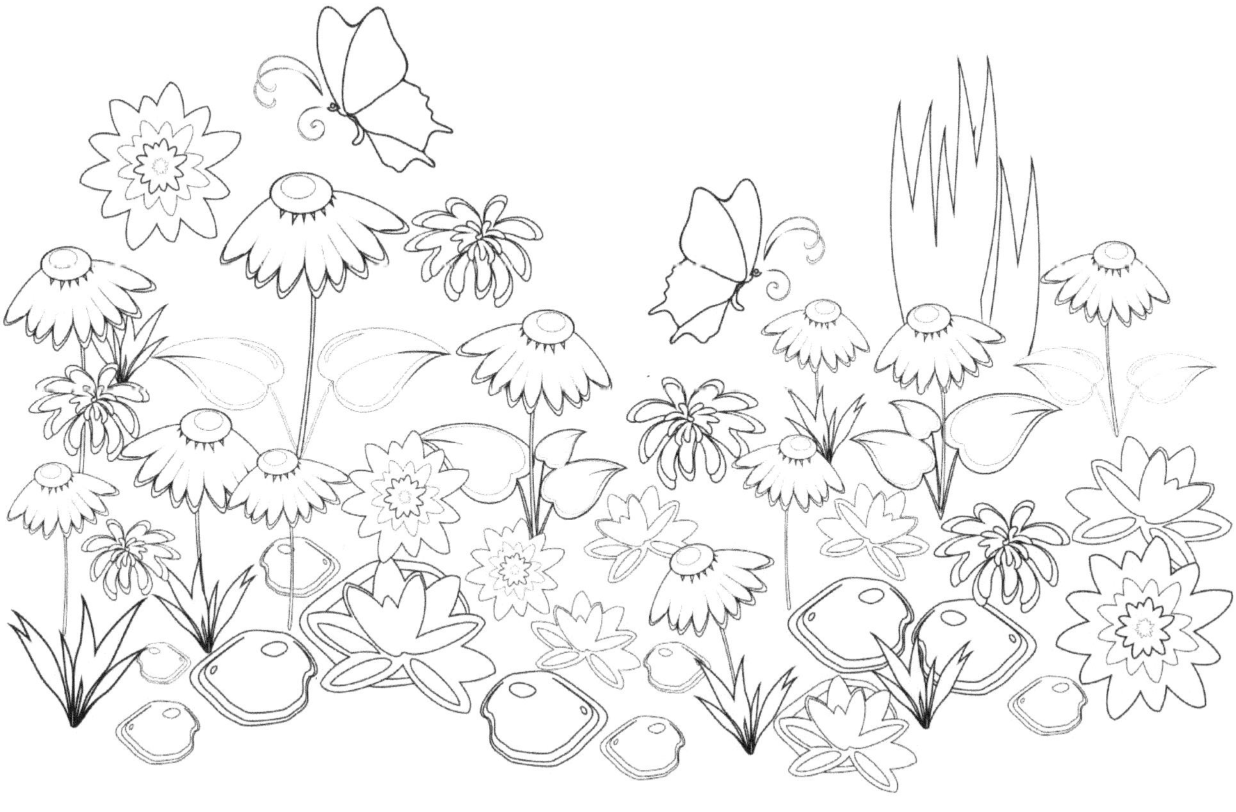

Rakel Olsson

Charming Paris

Adult Coloring Book

Inspire Creativity, Reduce Stress

ISBN-13: 978-1535124683
ISBN-10: 1535124687

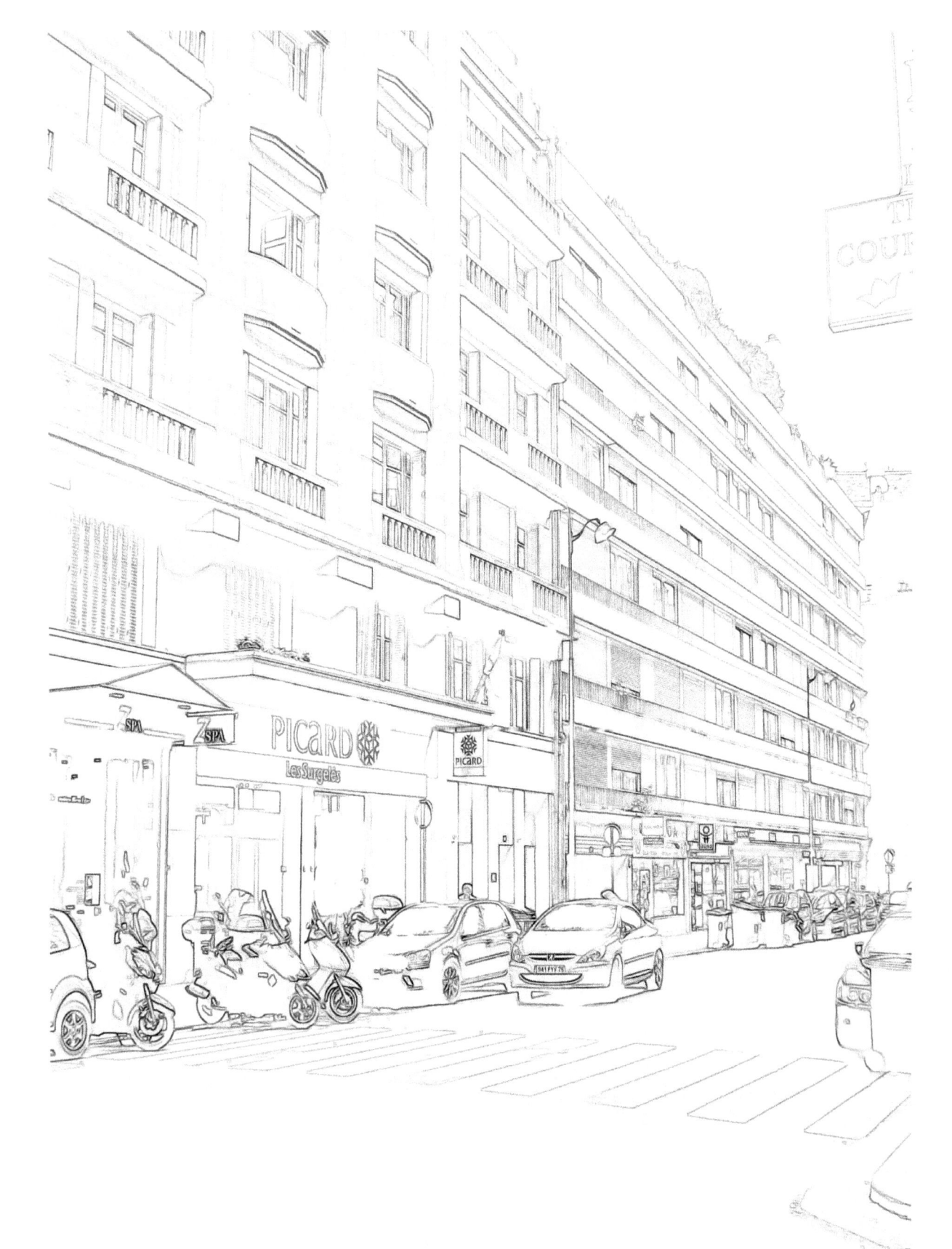

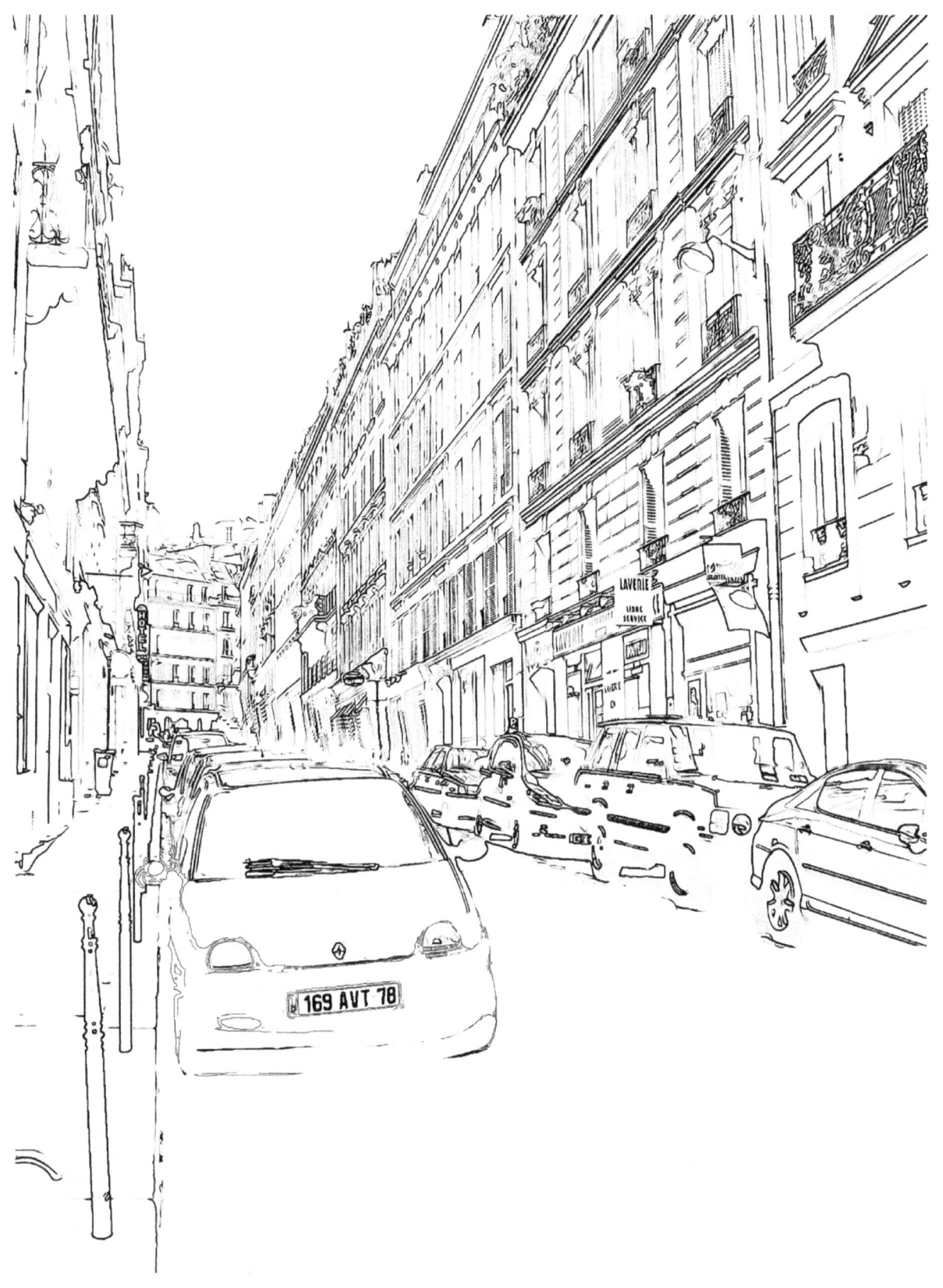

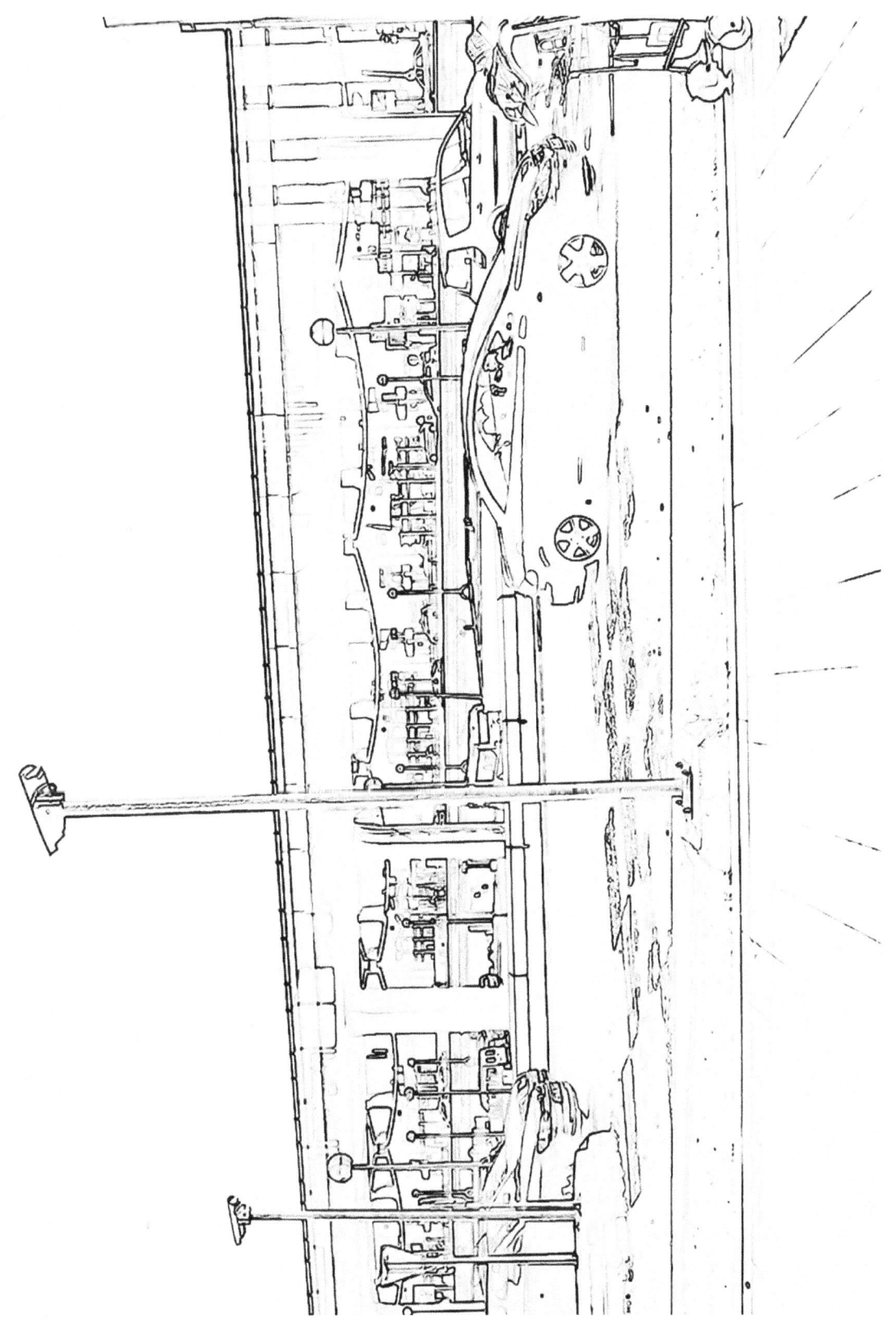

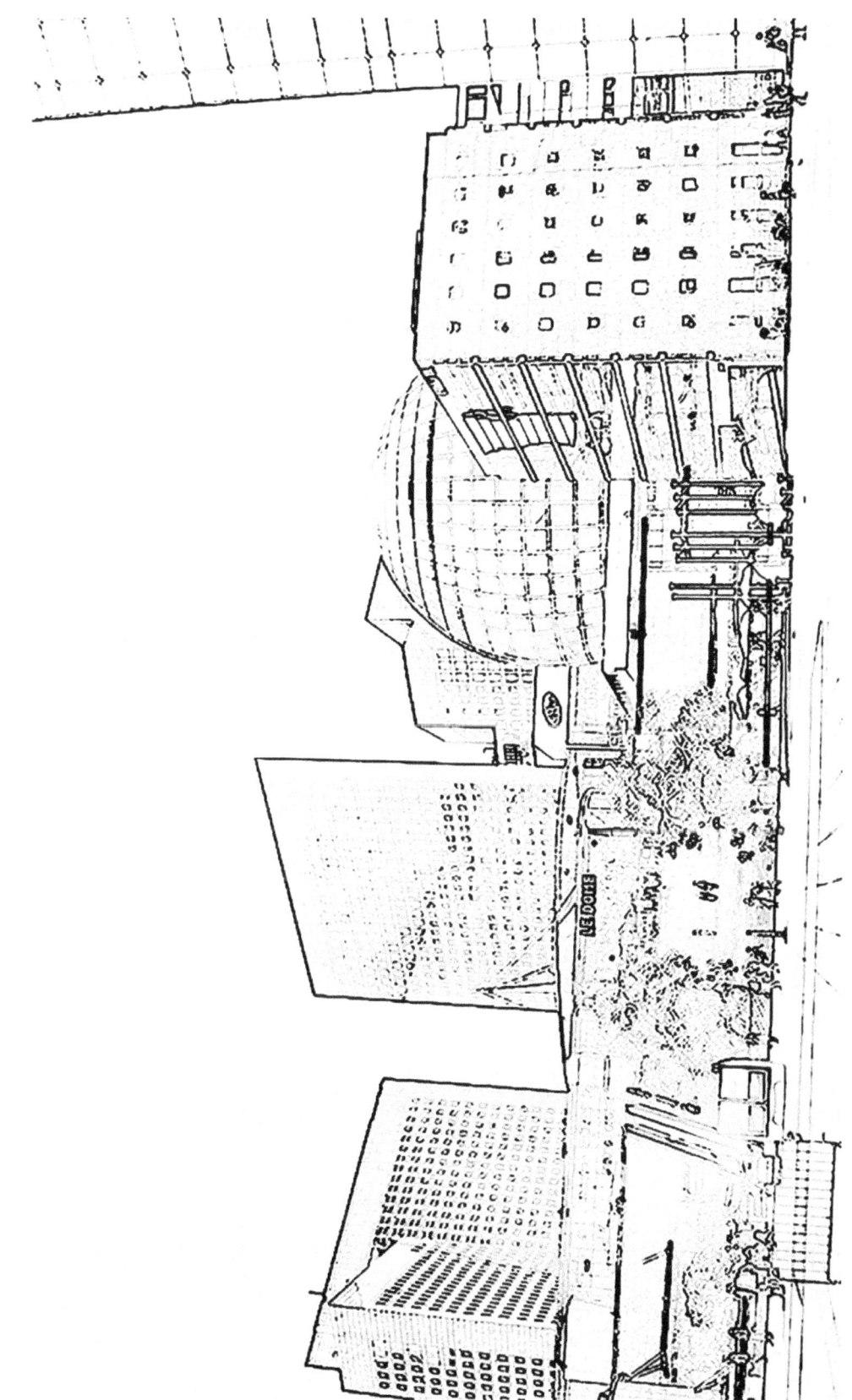

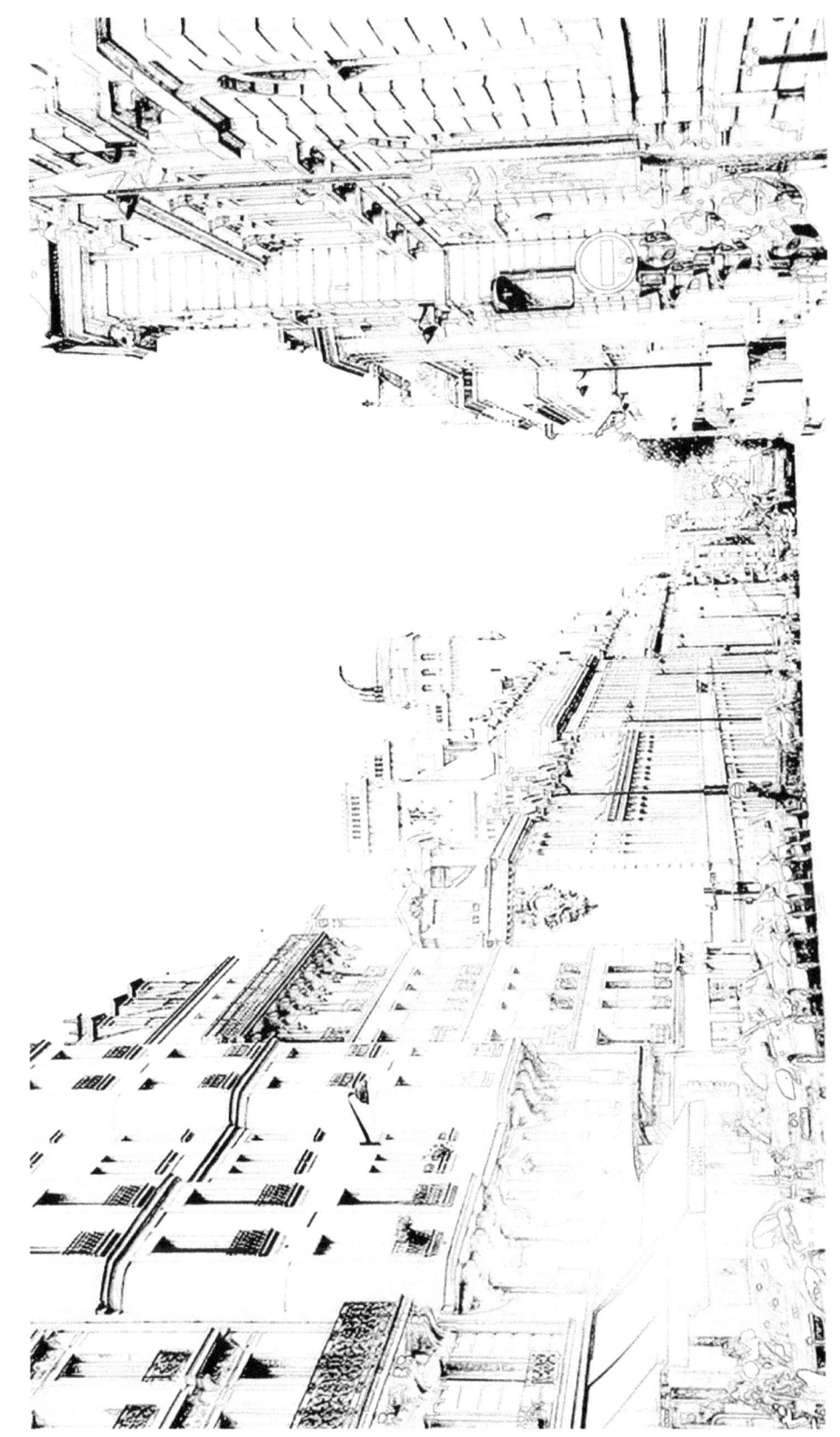

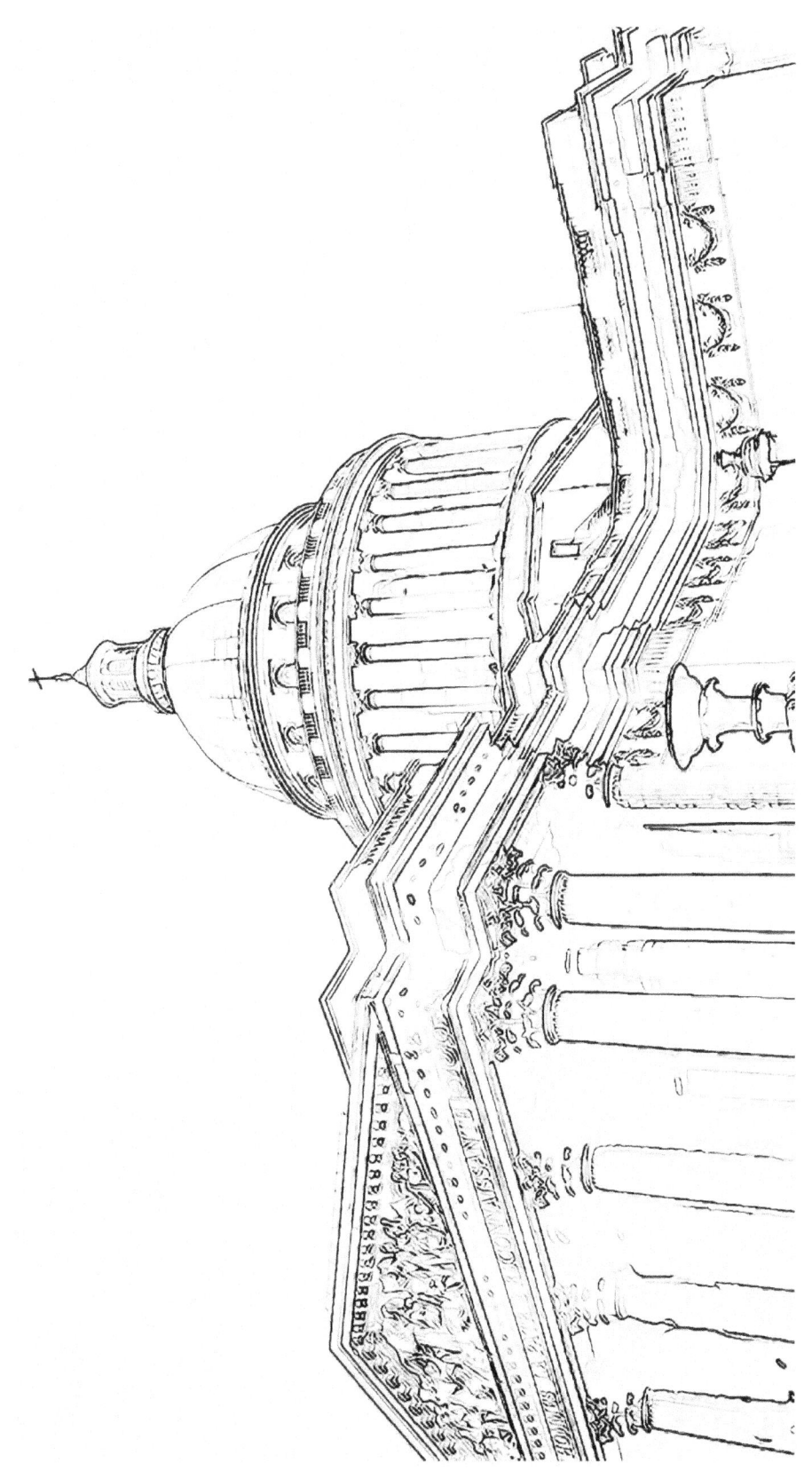

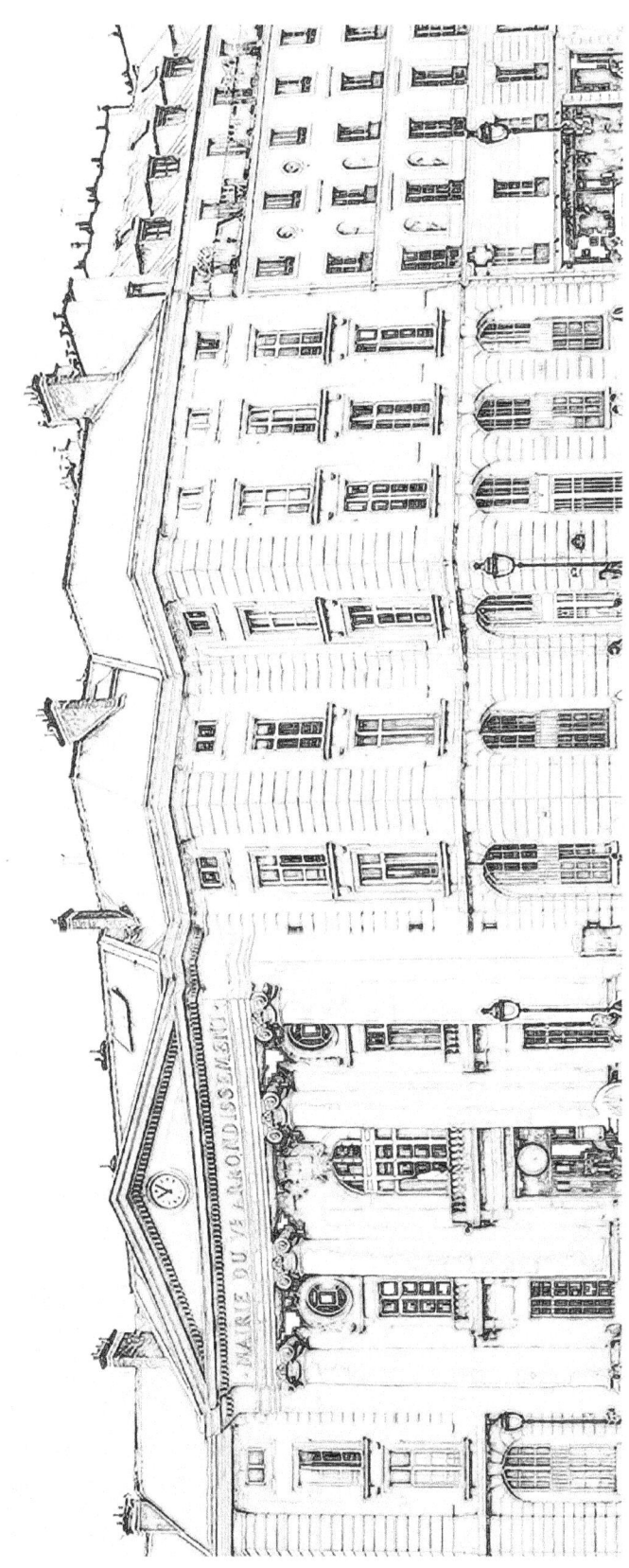

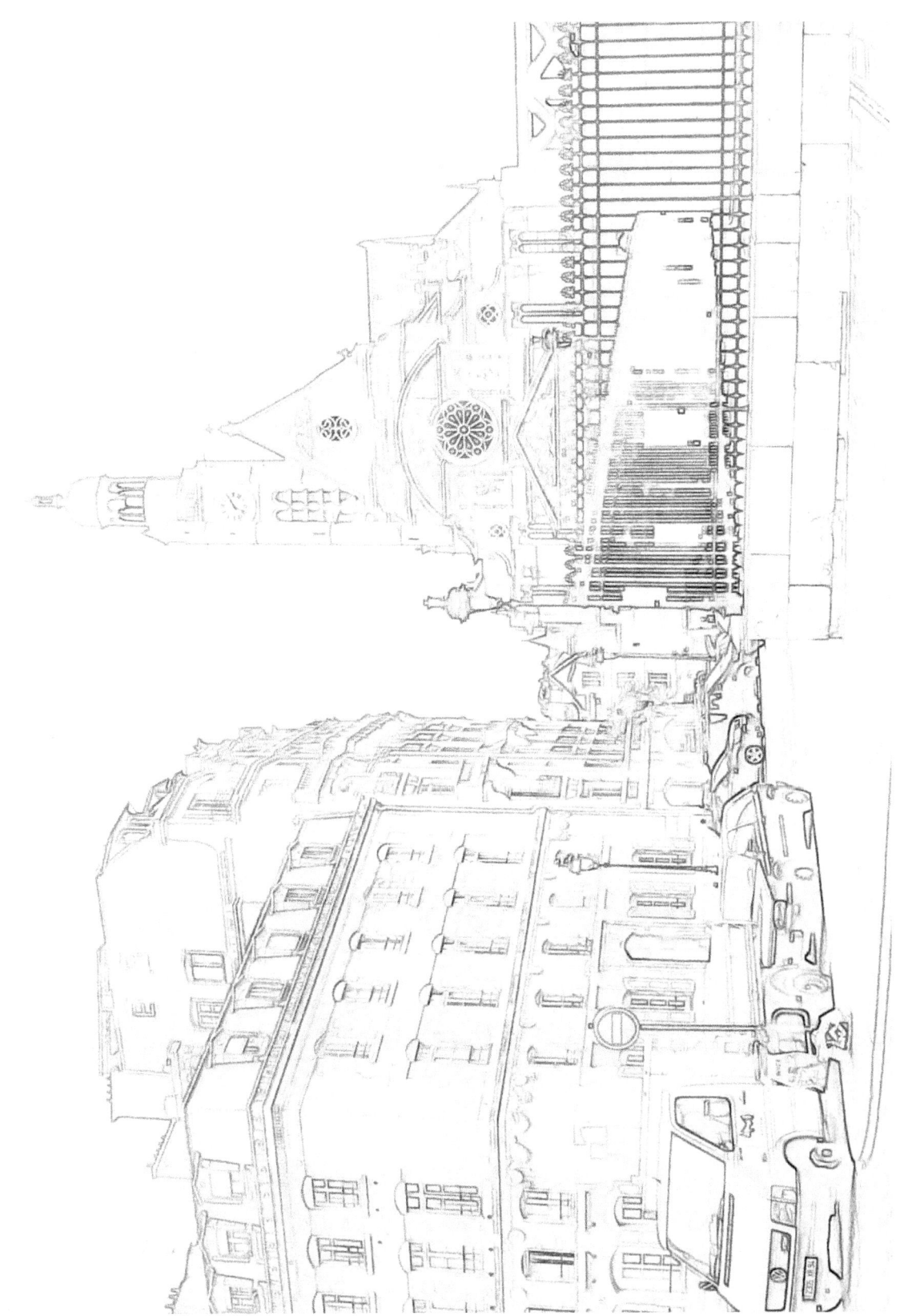

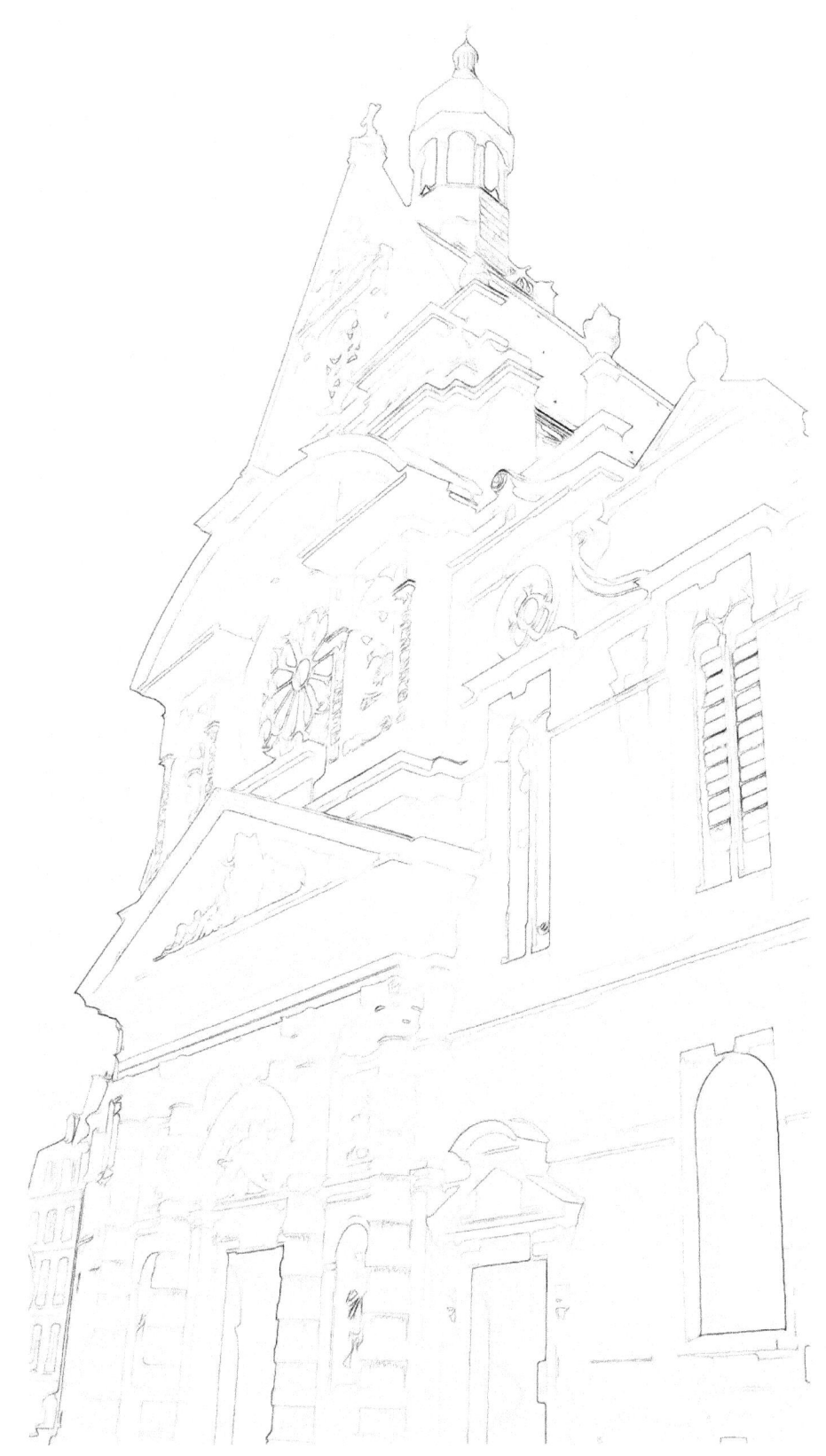

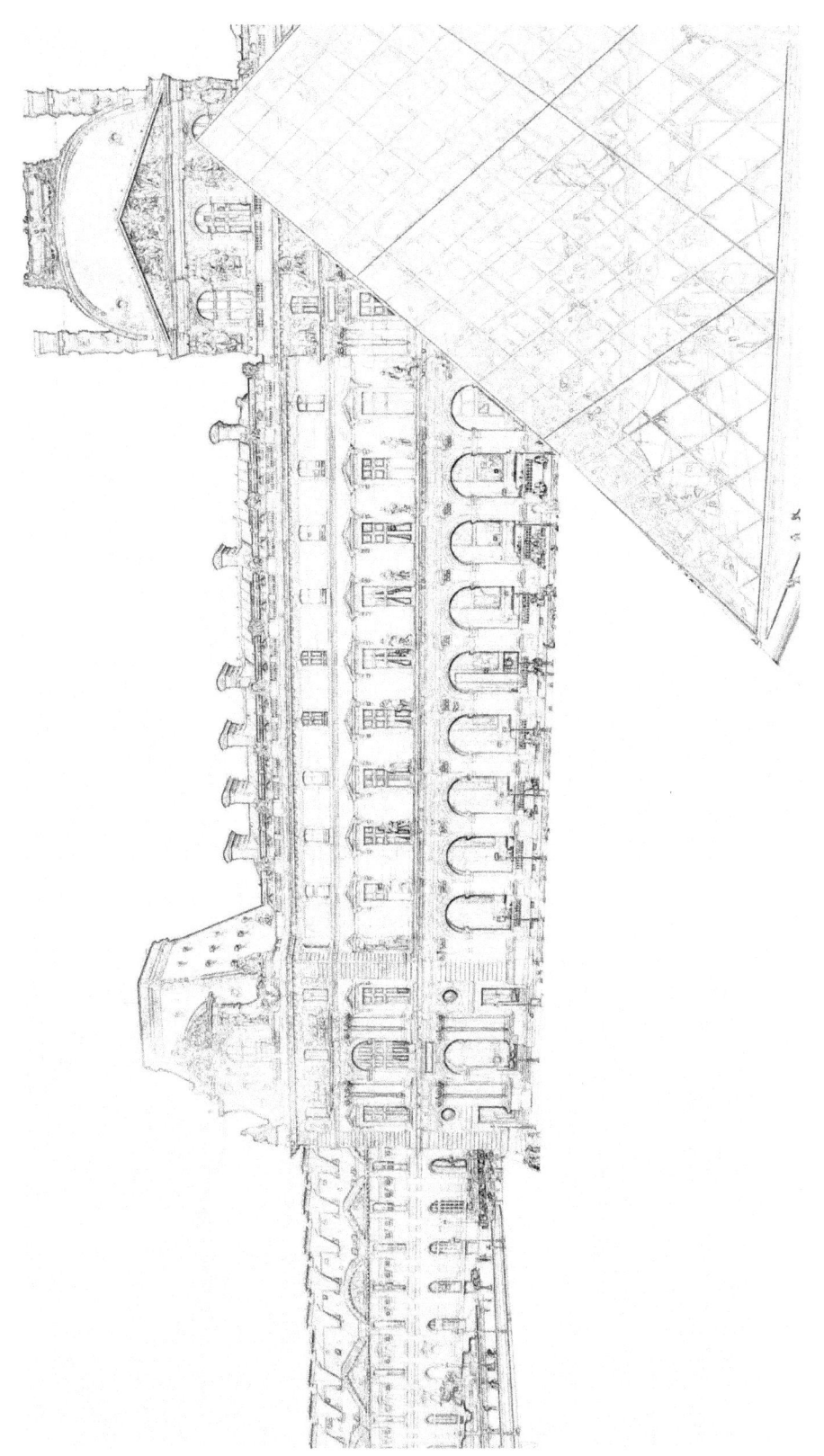

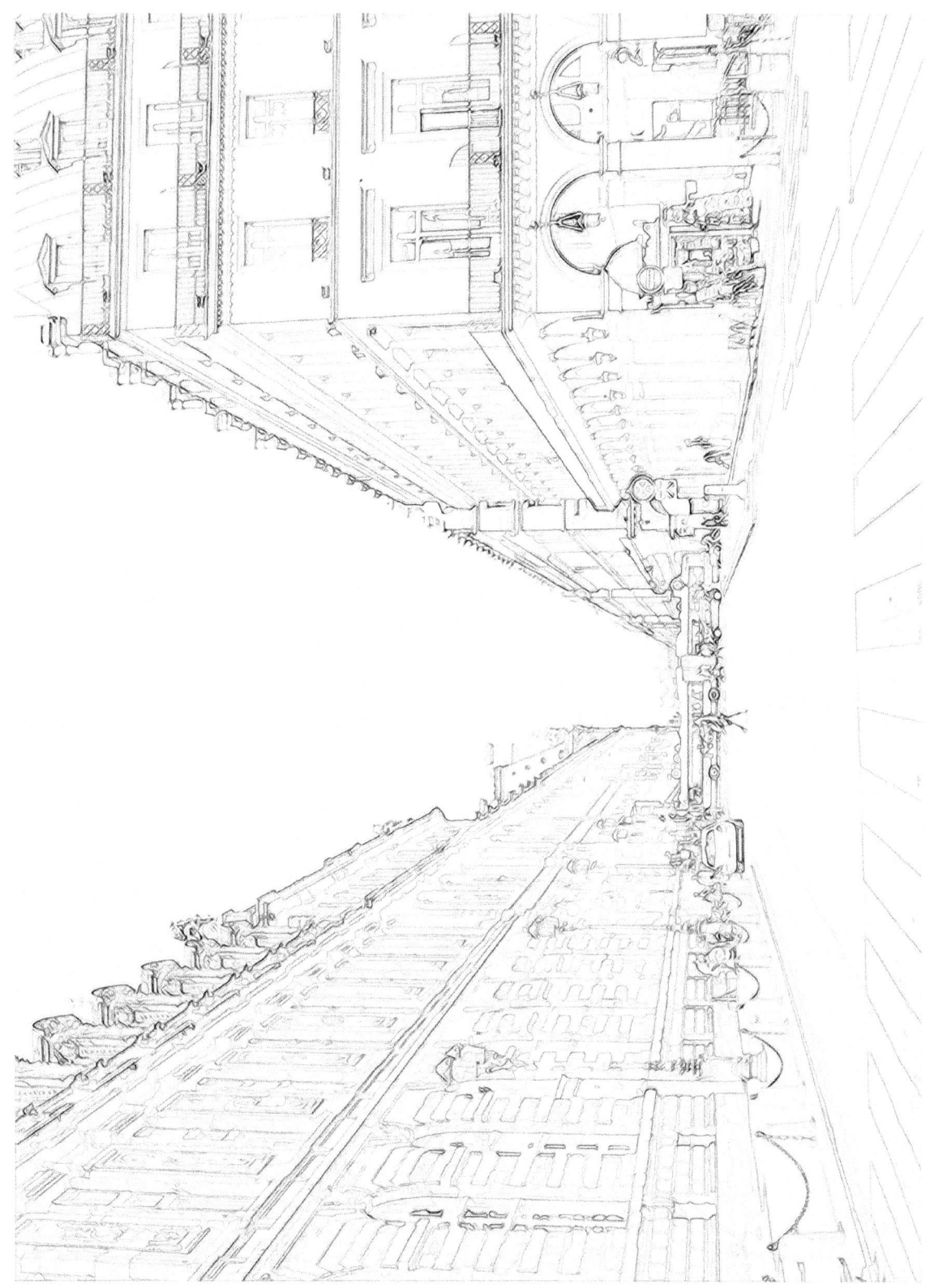

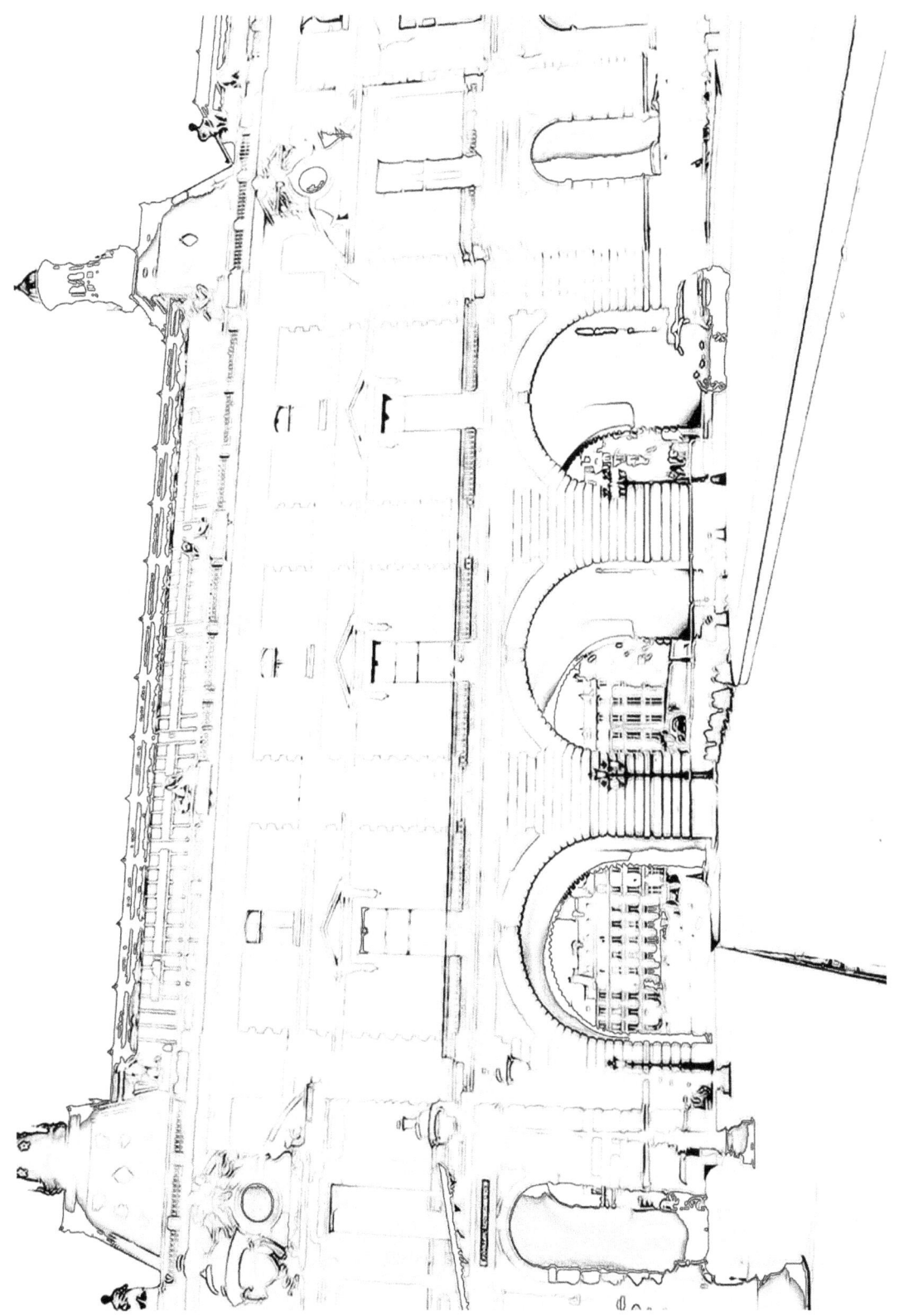

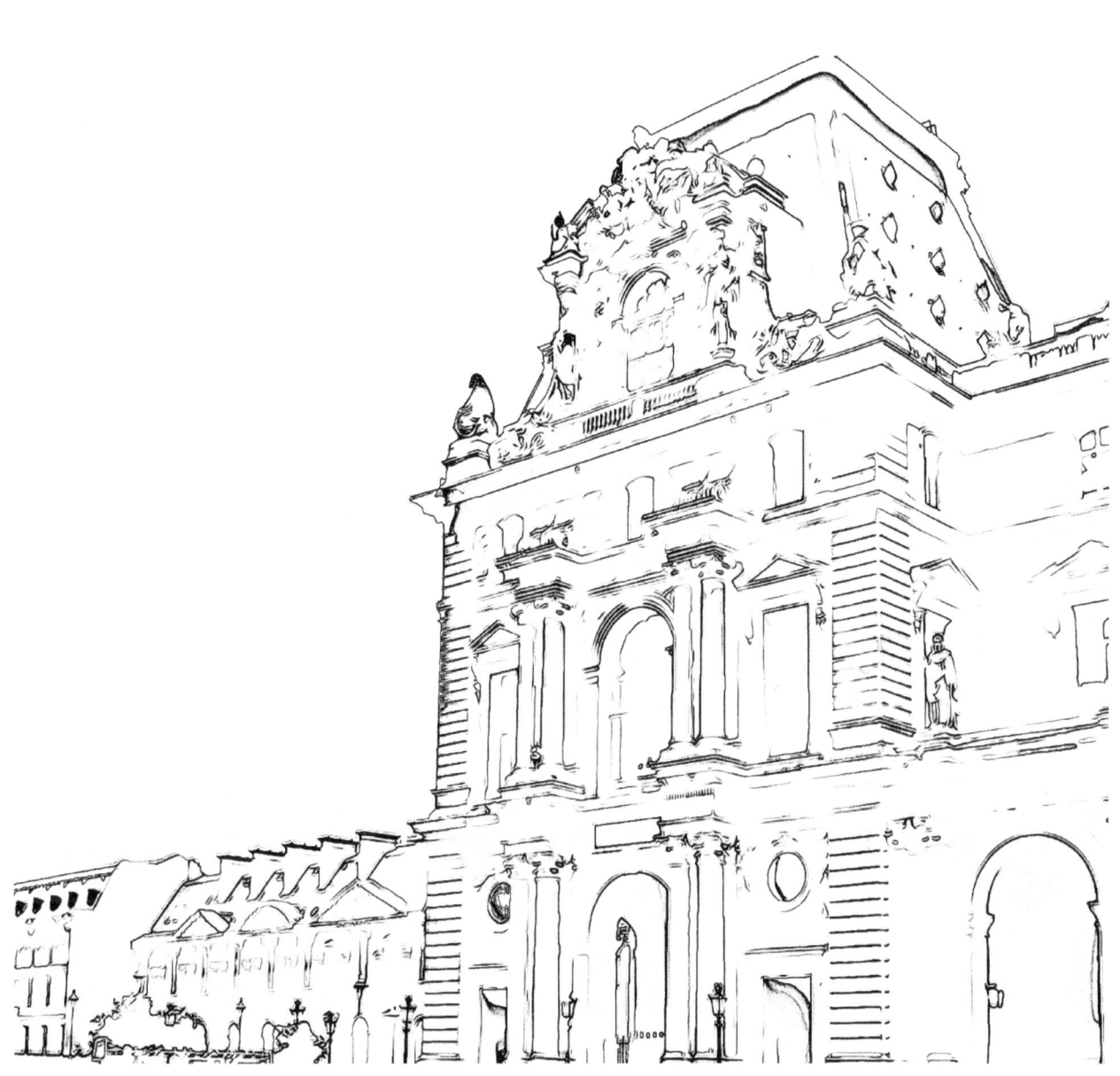

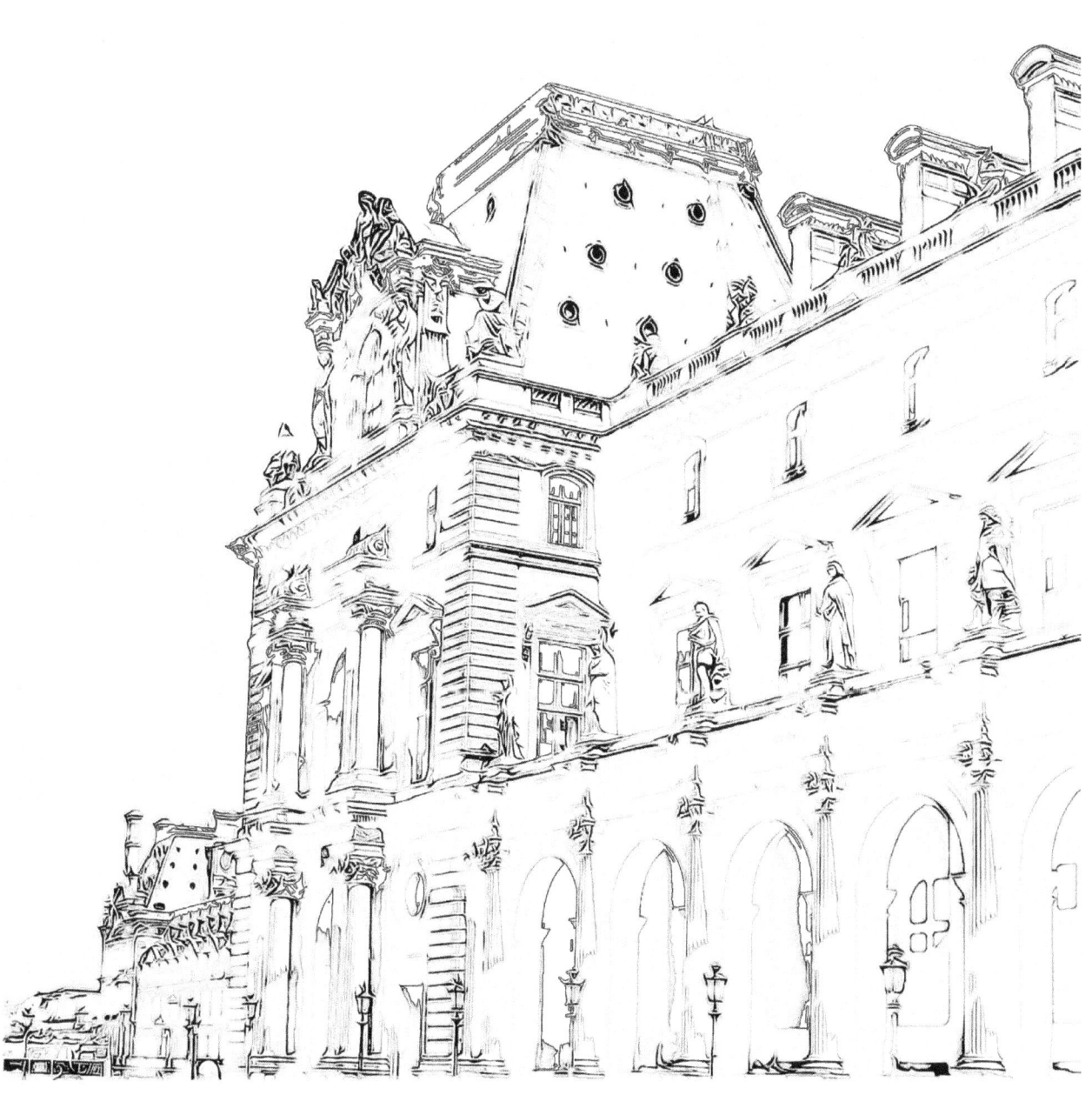

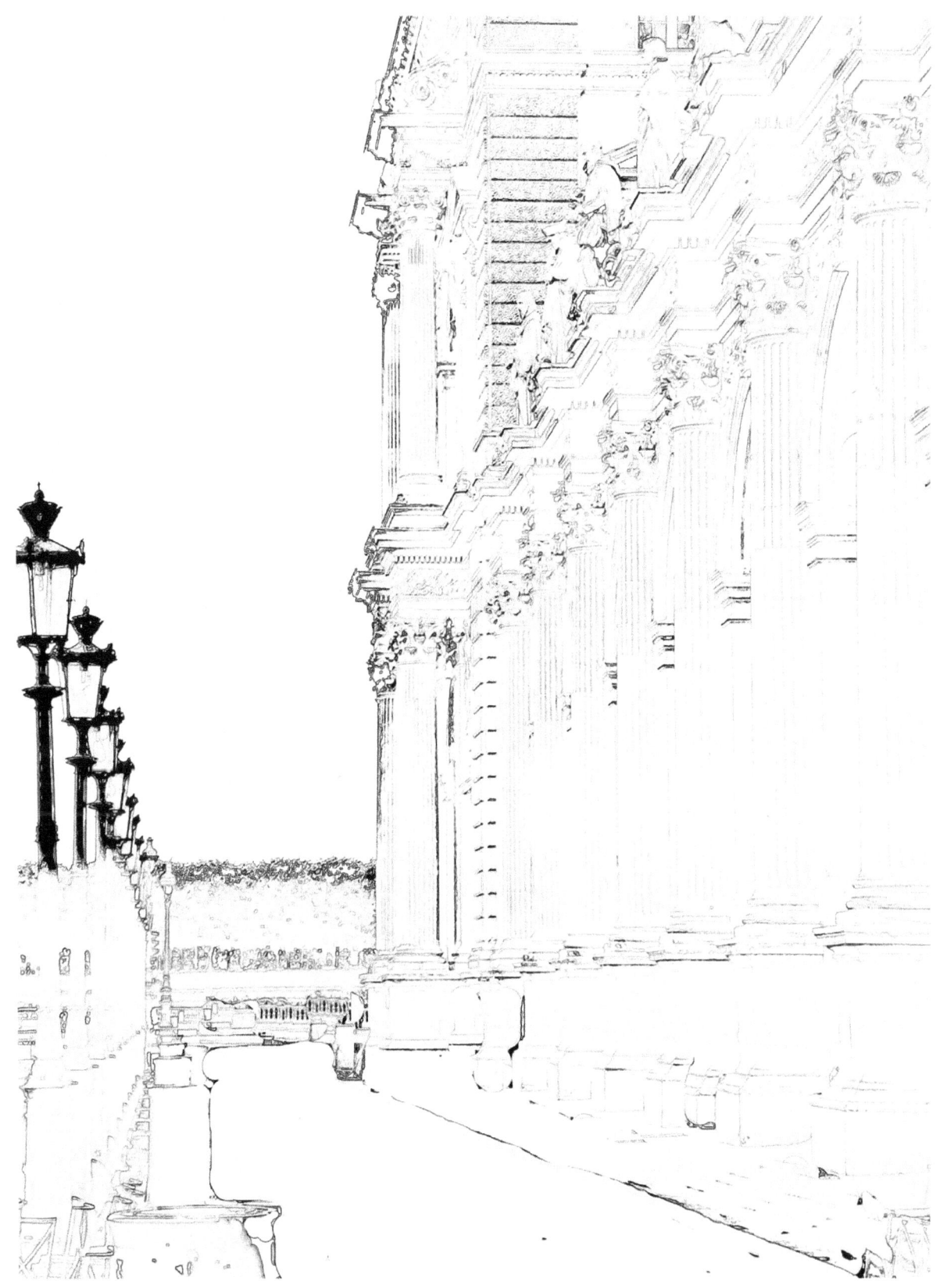

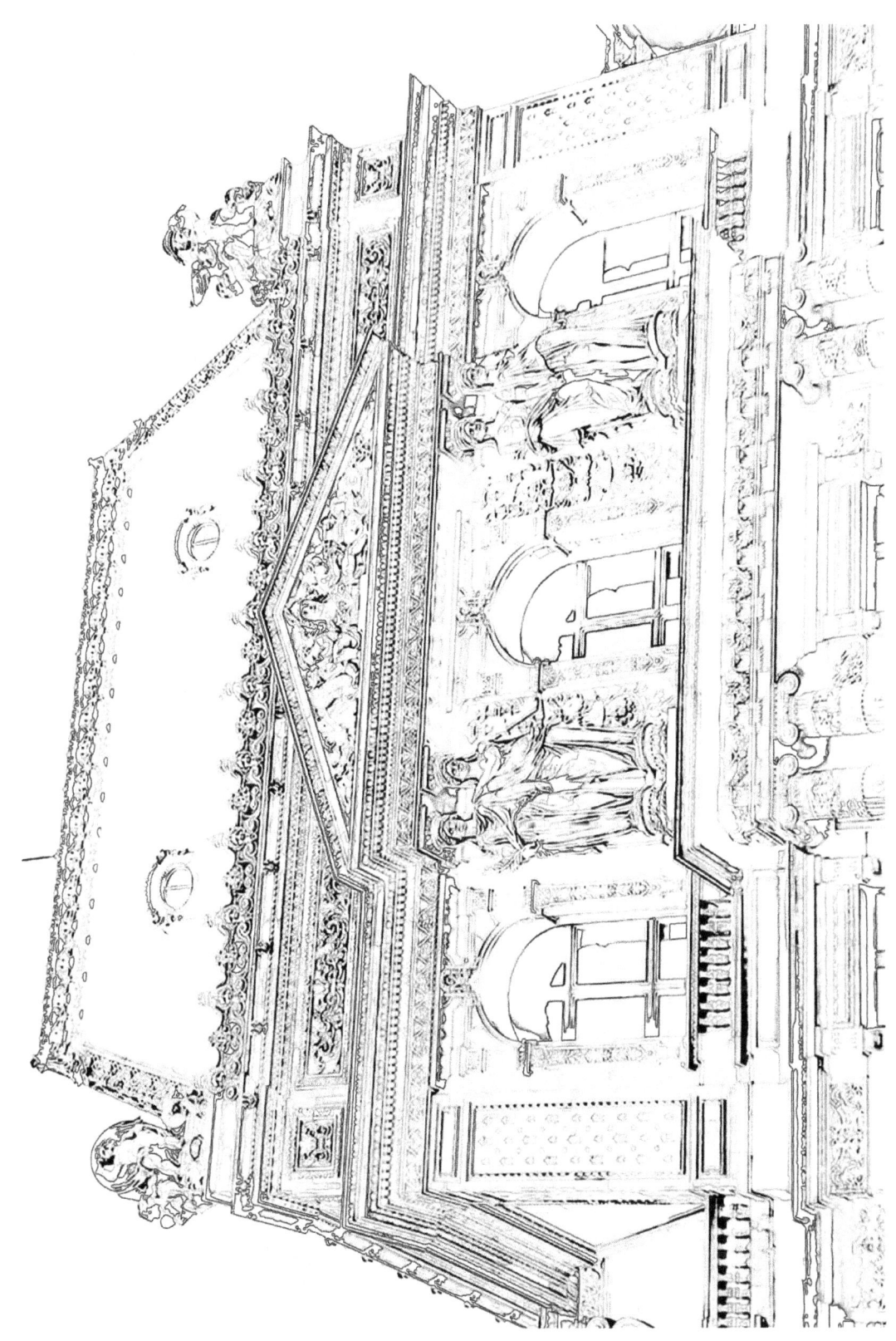

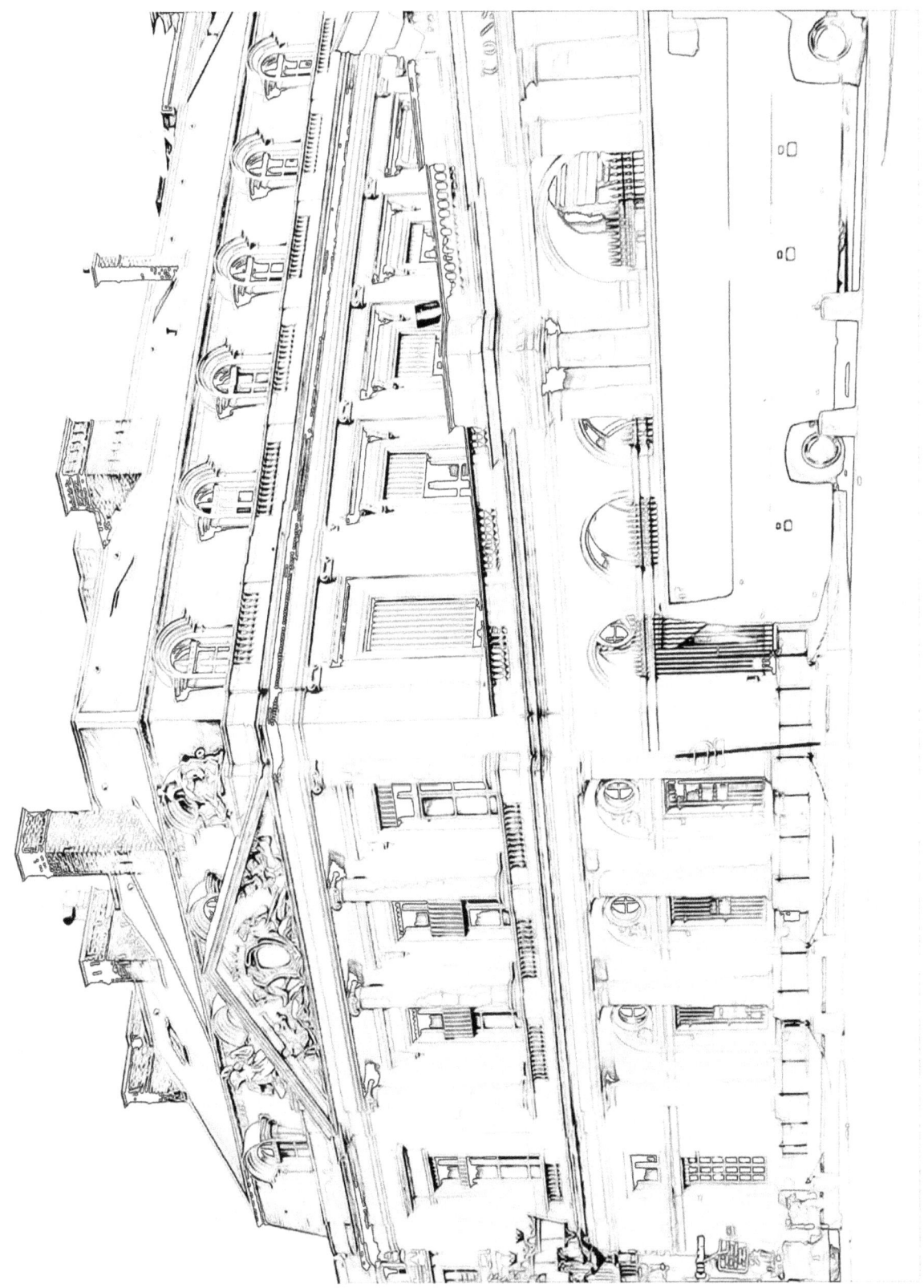

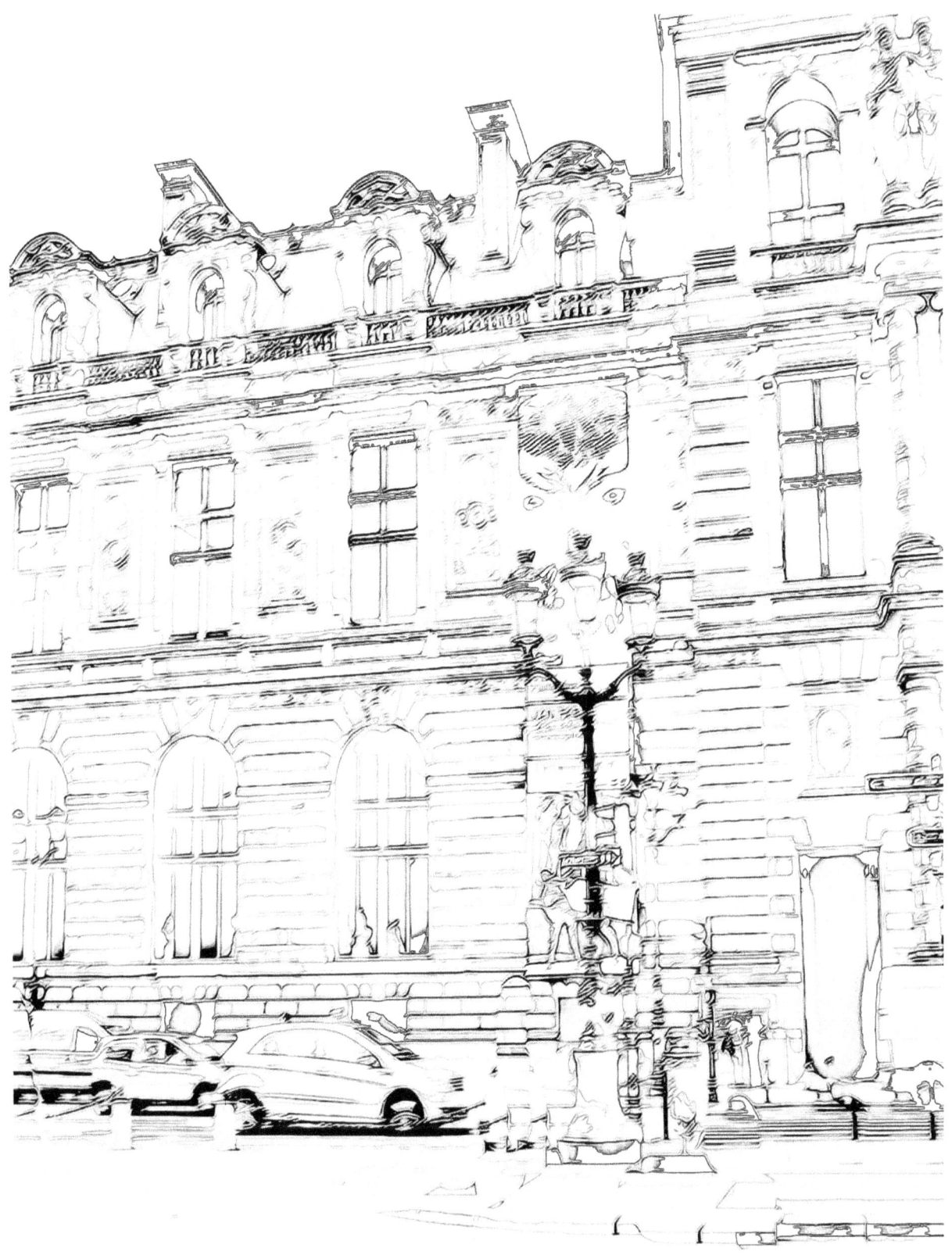

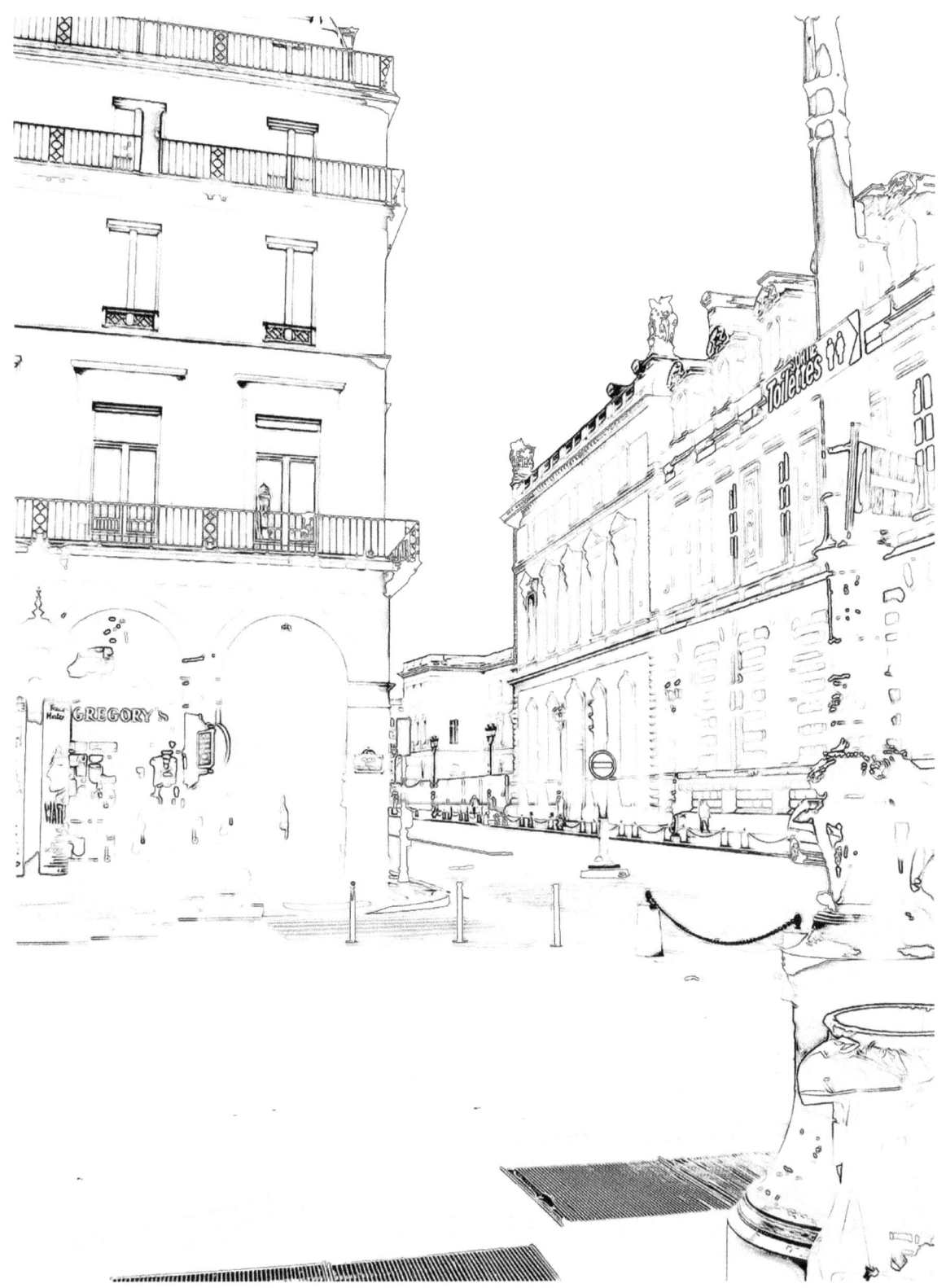

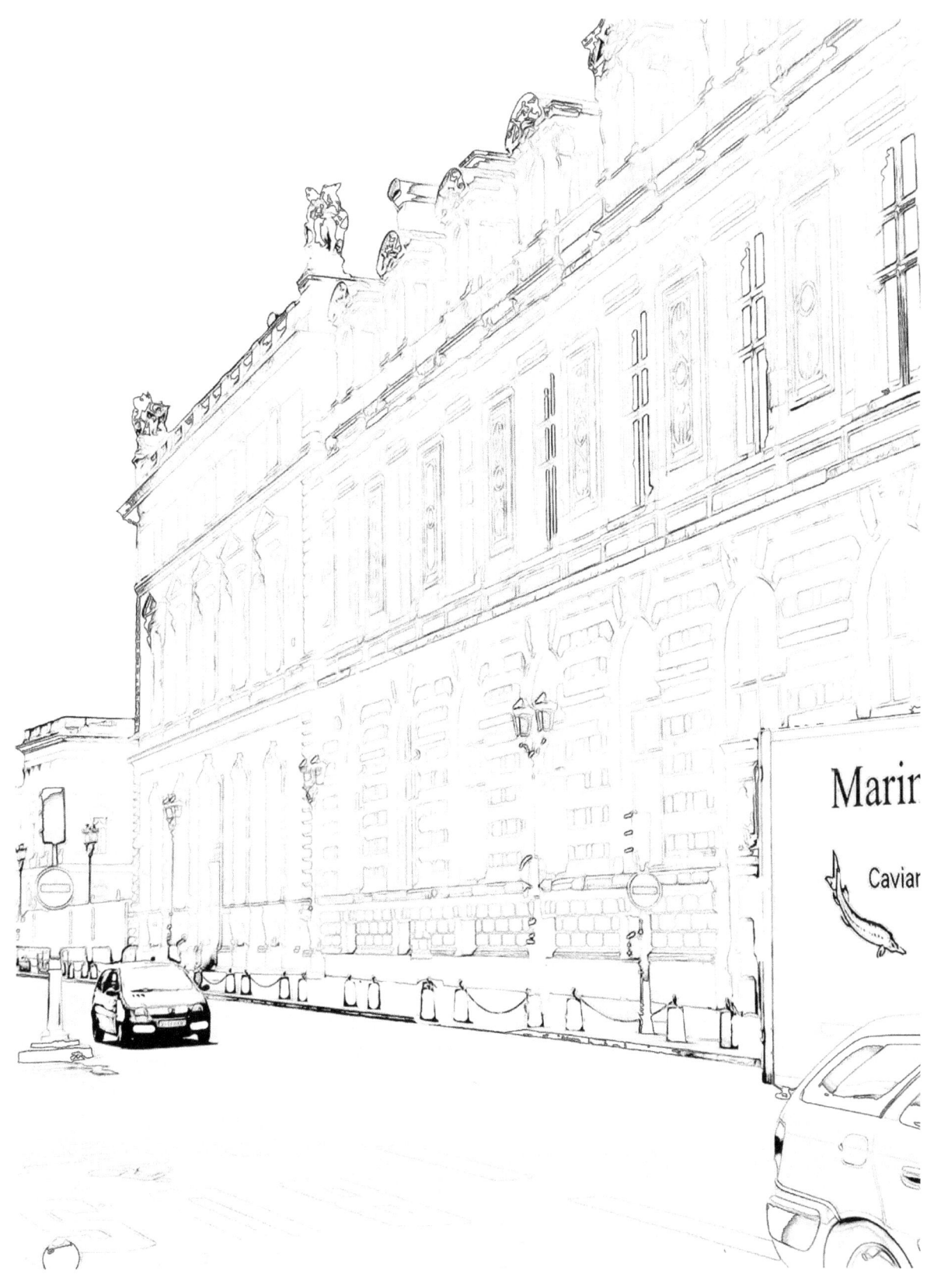

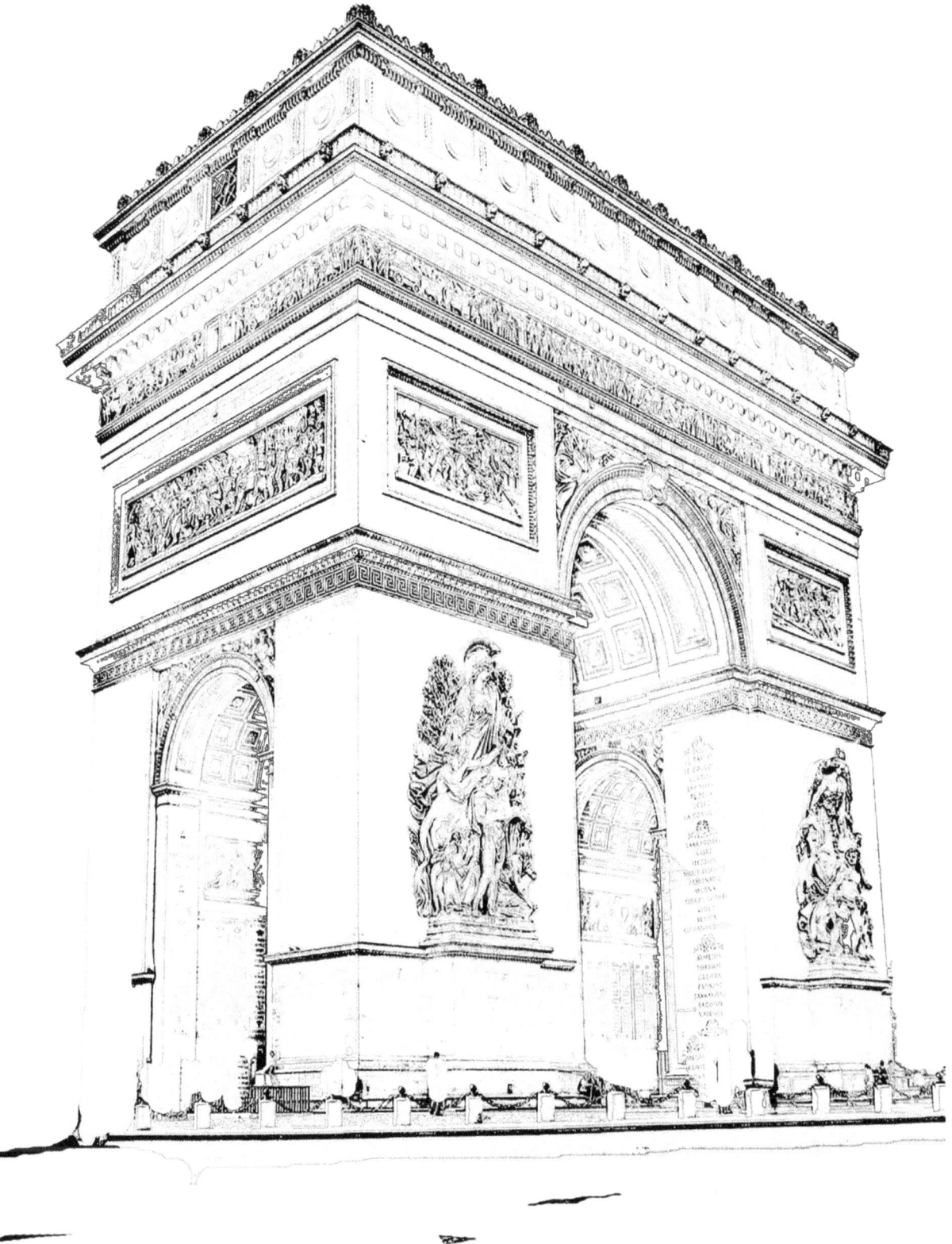

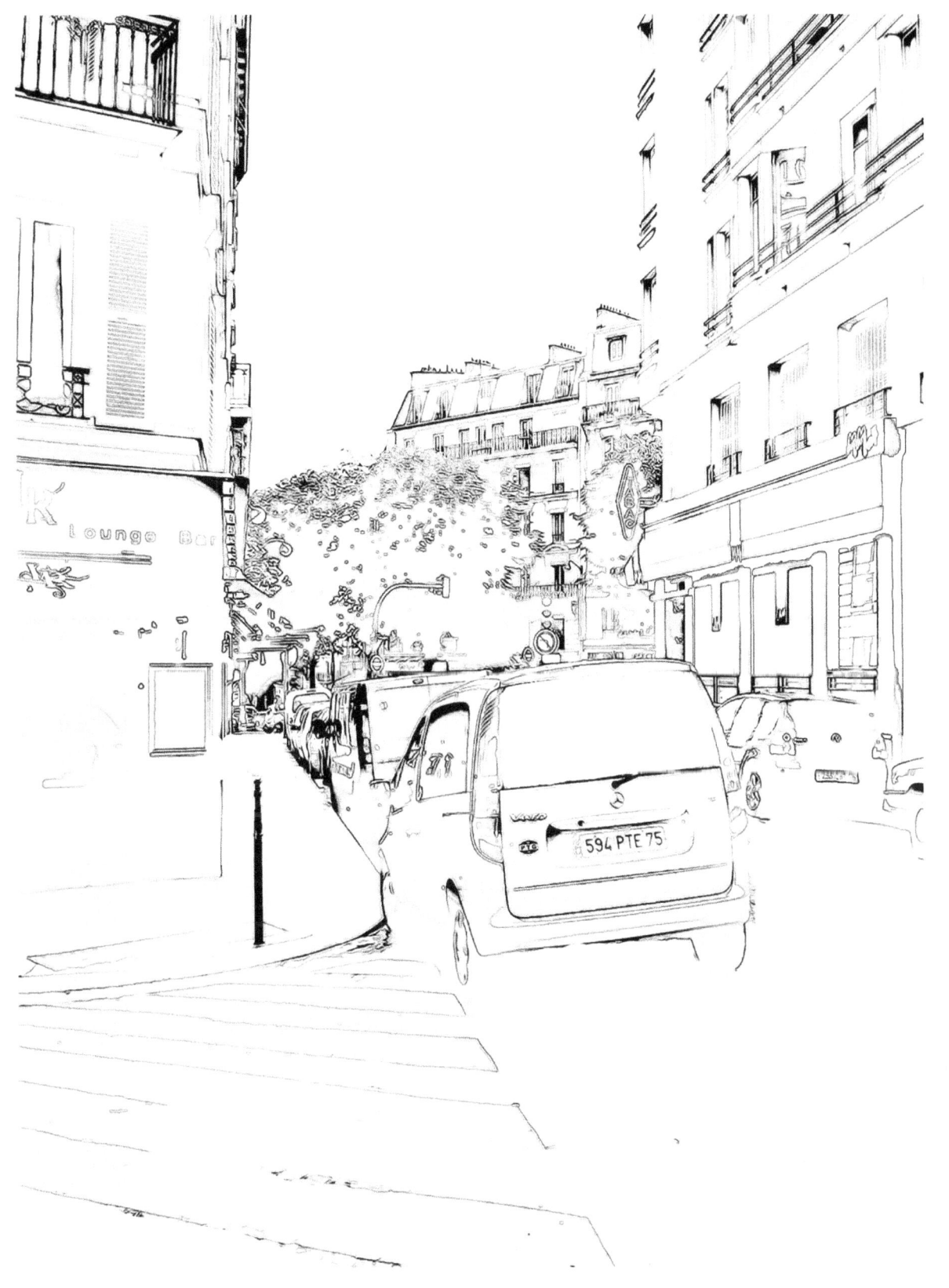

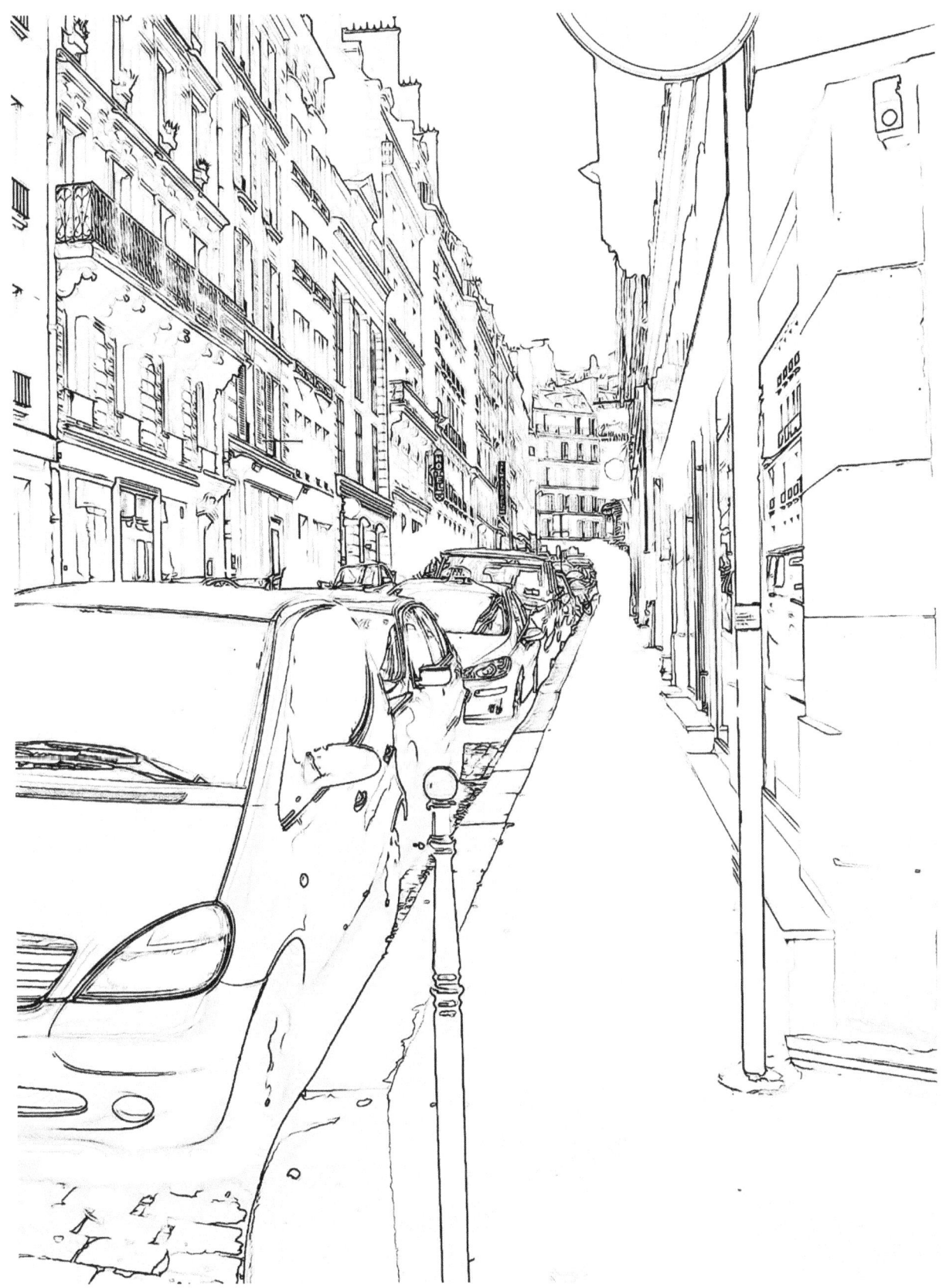

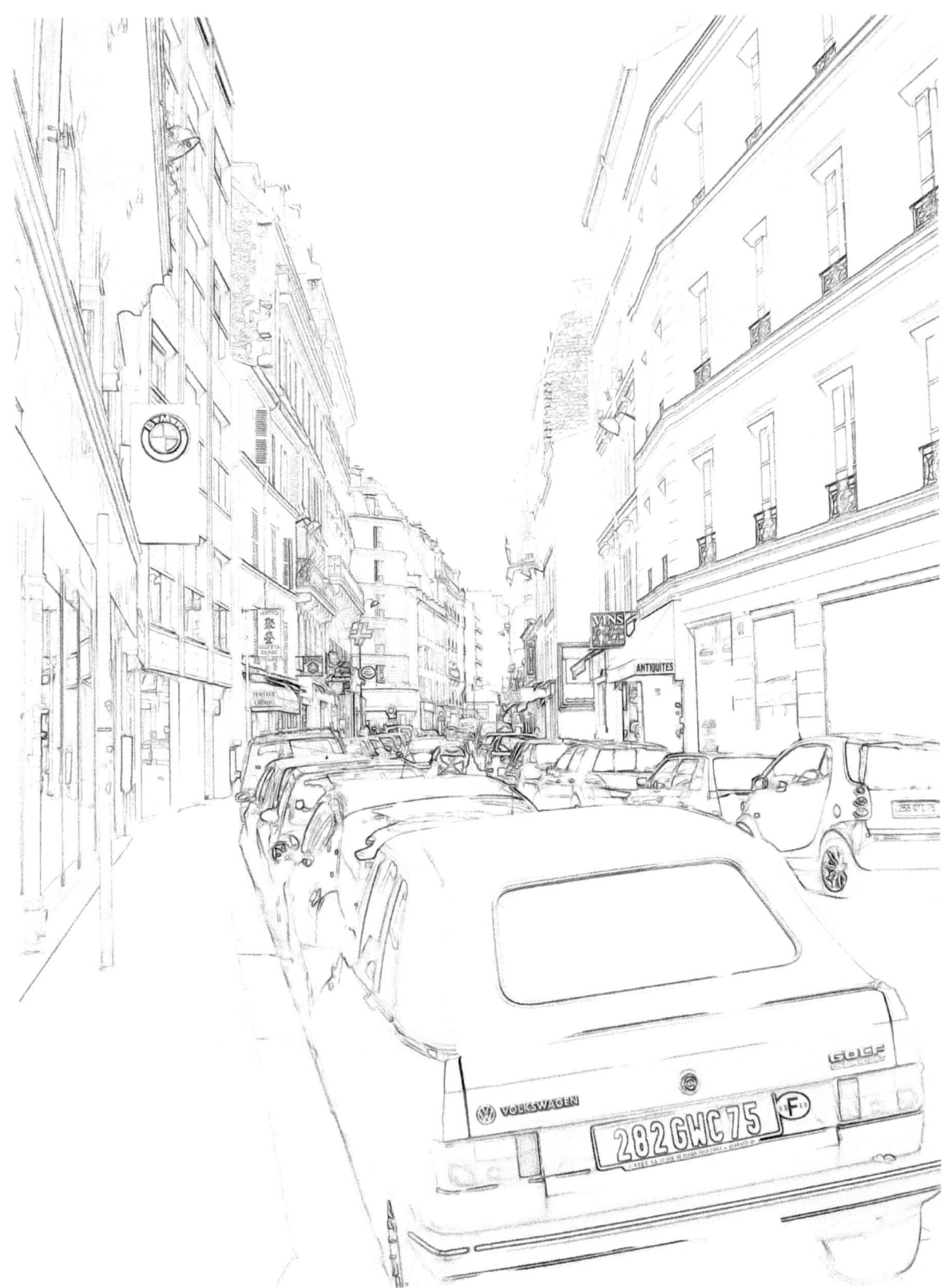

Thank you

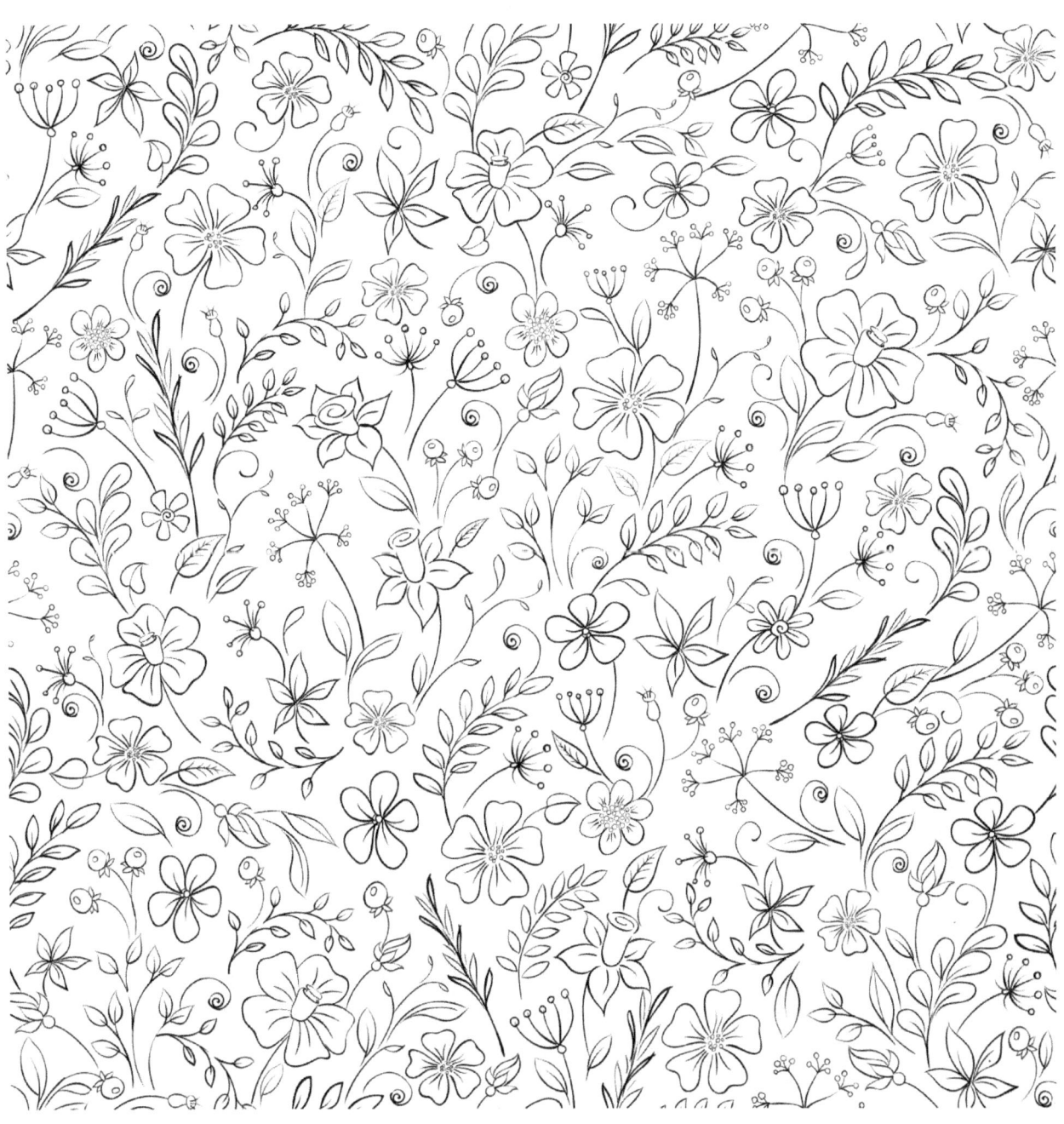

www.ingramcontent.com/pod-product-compliance
Lightning Source LLC
Chambersburg PA
CBHW080632190526
45169CB00009B/3370